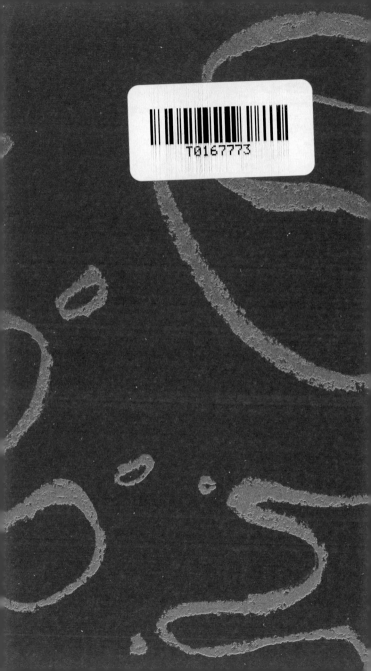

YOU ARE LOVED

NOW AGE ESSENTIALS

ESSENTIAL

YOU ARE

SPIRIT GUARDIANS

LOVED

AND GUIDES

CATHERINE BJÖRKSTEN

POP PRESS

1

Published in 2021 by Pop Press an imprint of Ebury Publishing,

20 Vauxhall Bridge Road,
London SW1V 2SA

Pop Press is part of the Penguin Random House group of companies
whose addresses can be found at global.penguinrandomhouse.com

First published by Pop Press in 2021

www.penguin.co.uk

A CIP catalogue record for this book is available from the British Library

ISBN 9781529107937

Typeset in 9/12 pt Neuzeit Office Pro
by Integra Software Services Pvt. Ltd, Pondicherry

Printed and bound in Great Britain by Clays Ltd, Elcograf S.p.A.

The authorised representative in the EEA is Penguin Random House Ireland,
Morrison Chambers, 32 Nassau Street, Dublin D02 YH68.

Penguin Random House is committed to a sustainable future for
our business, our readers and our planet. This book is made from
Forest Stewardship Council® certified paper.

Contents

AHO MITAKUYE OYASIN.
TO ALL MY RELATIONS.

Introducing the Power of Spirit Guides

Invocation

WELCOMING YOUR SPIRIT GUIDES

As you start reading these words, I call forward your Spirit Guides who are here to support and guide you through life on the Earth plane.

I call forward those who love you unconditionally and are of the Light in your ancestry, in the animal and plant kingdoms, gods and goddesses, nature and star allies.

May you open your heart to receiving the love and support you will need to live your highest potential on Earth.

You are a blessed child of the Universe who has come here to be seen for your greatest gifts and deserve to be honoured by all the realms you exist in.

Have you ever felt a breeze when there were no open doors or windows next to you? Have you caught the shape of 'someone' in the corner of your eye or had a deep knowing? What about a gut feeling for a situation or a person? Or have you ever experienced a spooky coincidence, such as seeing an advertisement on the side of a bus when you were asking yourself if you should go there on your next trip?

These are the nudges and the guidance that our Spirit Guides offer us on a daily basis. Our Spirit Guides are our spiritual crew who have our back while we are navigating life on Earth – they have been assigned to support you and their interest is to see you 'win' at life. Their purpose is to clue you in when you are lost, off-track or feel confused as to what's next; because Spirit Guides have mastered lessons that we are yet to go through in this lifetime on Earth and they want to support you in developing your highest potential – so that you feel confident, uplifted, excited and find an overarching sense of fulfilment.

My aim in *You Are Loved* is to help you connect with the unseen world of spirit. The spirit world will provide you with many allies or Spirit Guides for when you are in need of support in any areas of your life. We can often feel alone in this thing called Life and we can always turn to our Spirit Guides for assistance in the way that we already call on friends and family; you should see your Spirit Guides as an additional source of guidance – and surely that is something to be welcomed?

We will look into what and who Spirit Guides are, as well as how you can find and recognise them. You will learn how to spot the signs that your Guides are 'online'; how they reach you and how you reach them; in other words, how you can build a steady relationship with them.

What will You Discover with Your Spirit Guides?

Spirit Guides can help you to connect more deeply with your inner compass, which will support you in feeling more at peace and empowered with the decisions you make and the direction you take in life.

Connecting with your Spirit Guides will also sharpen your intuition, so you will trust yourself more and know that you have a guidance system that will support you in making choices that will put you on a life path that is more joyful and less stressful. When you follow the signs and listen to your heart, you cannot go wrong. Life will flow with more ease as you learn to trust yourself.

The 'mission' of your Spirit Guides is to remind you of your greatness. Your Spirit Guides will help you to get a better understanding of who you truly are. As you deepen your relationship with them, you will deepen your relationship with yourself, and you will uncover and remember aspects of yourself.

They are great allies to have when we are inquiring about our life path or purpose, answering questions such as: what have I come to do here on Earth? What job would fit best with my life purpose? What is the most supportive environment for me to live in – the buzzing and creative city, mellow country, cleansing sea, higher perspective mountain, or deep forest?

Spirit Guides can help us see what we can sometimes not see for ourselves: a person's intention, a higher perspective of a situation (such as potential job opportunities or a romantic relationship), or the energy of a living space such as a flat. Think of your Spirit Guides as 'multidimensional sounding boards' that you can use in everyday situations. This can take the form of questions relating to a person you are dating, a job offer you are considering or a new friend or housemate; from deciding what you are going to eat to whom you spend your time with; to living in which area will benefit you the most.

Ultimately, our Spirit Guides are training us to realise that we have an innate guidance system that will never fail us. They help us realise that we are like diamonds: multi-faceted and talented. They help us remember what comes to us with ease and grace, and what brings us joy, by pointing us in the right direction as we start working with them. They remind us that it is all already within us; we just need to remember.

Part of the experience that we have with our Spirit Guides is feeling that we are loved beyond measure, uncondi-tionally. No matter what we have done, we are held in deep love by our Guides. They know us better than anyone because they can see the purity of our soul and our capacity as humans. This is what they are here to remind us of. When you are feeling anxious or need a little push to step fully into your power and brilliance, they will be there, cheering, setting up signposts to guide you towards fulfilment, joy, love and success. What they ask of you is trust and faith.

What this Book Offers

This book will teach you how to become proficient in 'spirit speak', so that you can always get the support you need throughout life's ebbs and flows. And that, my dear reader, will be priceless. Learning how to bring in your Guides will expand your relationship with life and provide you with resources and support that you didn't know you had. We are, after all, interconnected – humans, animals, plants, trees, stars – the entire cosmos. When they say that you are an expression of the Universe, you really are.

I will show you how to connect with your Guides and build a relationship that will enhance your intuition, your trust in yourself and in the Universe; you will understand that you are not alone and are always supported. As you feel this support from your Guides, you will develop a sense of safety within yourself that will give you the confidence to navigate pretty much any situation that presents itself. When you know that you can rely on your intuition, you know that you can rely on yourself. You will need less external validation and approval from others, because you will know what is right for you. And this trust will, ultimately, bring you a more peaceful and fulfilling life.

My Spirit Guides have helped me rekindle my trust in myself and remind me who I am, giving me much-needed confidence. When I have moments of doubt in life, I now check in with my Guides. I have learned how to drop into my body, still my mind and open my heart to connect with them as a navigation system for all situations in life that require decision-making.

I feel much stronger physically, mentally, emotionally and energetically too, because I know that I have back-up from the highest realms and because I know that my highest interest, even when I cannot see it myself, is the 'endgame'. It has been a huge lesson for me to trust in myself, others and the Universe, and I have learned to be kinder to myself as well as to stop pretending to be someone else. As I trust myself and love myself more, I can now love and trust others more, and I have moved from a vicious circle into a virtuous circle.

I hope that you will find a renewed life force and a source of energy to create the life you have always wanted and deserve. Connecting with your Spirit Guides is an essential step on the road to Awakening, because it is how you will understand that you are much more than you believe yourself to be. There is more to this life than what you have been told and taught. Mind, body, spirit – remember? This is why having your own experience of spirit is so important; it will help you see your life and yourself in a wider perspective, open to all available opportunities.

And, by caring for ourselves energetically, looking after our mental well-being and understanding that we are part of nature, we can integrate spirituality into our daily lives, which is great news!

Lastly, getting connected to your body through movement, dance, singing, yoga and getting out into nature is a great thing for both your physical and mental health.

Your body is a fantastic source of wisdom. Listen to it because it always knows. When you start aligning all your facets and integrating spirit, you will receive love, wisdom and clarity as you venture out into the world to shine your brightest light and be seen for the wonderful limitless being you have come here to be.

What are
Spirit Guides?

Firstly, let me explain where Spirit Guides reside. Some Guides live on the Earth plane, and therefore have a form that we can relate to – including nature spirits such as the elements (Earth, Fire, Water and Earth), plants (flowers and trees), animals and rocks (stones, mountains and crystals). These, we can, for the most part, touch, hear, smell and taste.

We also have Spirit Guides who do not have form, i.e. do not have a physical body, but an energy body. They range from a vibratory field that is more or less close to a physical incarnation; ancestors and spirit animals have a fairly close form to what we might recognise because we have seen and identified them with our five senses.

There are also Guides throughout human history that once took a human form and are now recognised as leaders or deities in established religions or cultures. These include figures such as Buddha, Jesus/Yeshua and Muhammad, for example. They are bridges between human and a higher form of consciousness.

If you look back over human history, you'll see many kinds of Guides, sometimes referred to as gods and goddesses. Guides have walked the earth for millennia, and each with a different purpose and special power. I won't speak about all these belief systems in this book because they are sacred to cultures that are not my own but I urge you to read about them yourself and understand the importance of these Spirit Guides.

In this book I will refer to what others might call God or the Divine, for example, as The Source. It is from The Source that all Guides come. It has no known shape and appears to different people in different ways. The Source, and each energy body that comes to Earth from it, has important lessons to share with us if we take the time to listen and understand them.

Spirit Guides are here to help you with your life lessons – they will help you to evolve – in my experience often in very practical ways that can help daily life! For example, if you want to meet a life or business partner your Guides can help you, guiding you through life lessons that will set you on the path to meet that person. Guides will support you through a few life lessons that will align you with this meeting of minds and/or hearts. Spirit Guides will offer you the opportunity, and in return, you will need to do the work. Lesson first, manifestation for your highest good comes as a result.

How We Connect with Spirit Guides

I believe that everything is fundamentally made from energy, frequency and vibration. As an example, think about music. You know it is there because you can hear it – but can you touch it? No. How about scents? Wi-Fi? The same. We know these things exist although they have no physical form that we can see with our eyes or touch with our hands.

To connect with the Spirit Guides, we need to use other senses than the ones we might be used to. We connect with spirit through intuition; you might have heard of someone talking about 'vibes' and this is the same thing. Everything gives off vibes, including people and places. I'm sure you have experienced that before. Some people or places feel warm, cosy and inviting, while others don't feel quite as good; you've heard the saying that 'something is giving me the creeps' ... Always listen to those gut-based feelings; they are messages from your unseen Spirit Guides and they will never fail you. We can pick up on the unseen because we live in a quantum field of consciousness that we are all connected to and a part of – the seen and the unseen; humans and spirits.

Connecting with your Spirit Guides is like connecting to your heart; it is not a mental or cerebral exercise. Actually, the more you try to figure it out and understand it versus feeling it, the more blocked and frustrated you might become. This is an invitation to trust your knowing, intuition and gut. To cultivate your heart connection, you need to train yourself to tune in to vibes.

This can be done by closing your eyes when you are in a place and just recognising how you feel there. Your body will 'speak'. You can also close your eyes while you are sitting comfortably at home and tune in to the energy around you. Notice what arises in your body, if you see any images or hear any voices. You will feel your Guides – sense them – without physically seeing them. You are essentially switching operating systems to connect with them. To get comfortable with your new MO, you will need to practise; experience will bring you clarity and trust in your own ability to communicate with your Spirit Guides.

I also refer to a spiritual Awakening, by which I mean making the choice to live consciously, understanding and accepting the world of Spirit Guides as an integral part of our human experience; and that we are multidimensional beings who exist on many planes, our physical expression being only one aspect of who we truly are. A spiritual Awakening means taking an interest in transforming our relationship with ourselves, and therefore with others. It is about starting to become curious as to who we are beyond what we have always known and been told by our cultural and societal norms.

How can We Communicate with Them?

Based on the premise that everything is made of energy and spirit is a lighter/faster form of energy than we are used to here in physical form, we need to have translation points for our contact with spirit. We can build a physical space for them at home or in a favourite or special place in nature, or travel to an energetically charged place (I'll go into more detail on calling your Guides later in the book.)

When we want to engage with our Spirit Guides, we need to invite them in; they are not allowed to intervene if we don't call upon them. It might take a little time to create a direct line to your Spirit Guides as both sides get used to communicating with each other. And it will also take some time to get used to reading the signs and trusting the voices (spirit versus self-doubt). In my experience, it is – like pretty much every skill we want to develop – a question of practice and consistency.

Like people, there are many types of guide and not every Spirit Guide is for everyone. By building our spiritual connection with time and through practice, we get a better understanding of whom we are compatible with and whom we trust and communicate well with. Sounds familiar? Working with the spirit world is like working on human relationships. First you take the leap, next you speak to the spirit and then you will get the confirmation and answer to your question.

What do Spirit Guides Offer?

Life can be intense, and we all need support along the way. Our friends and families usually have our best interests at heart and can offer guidance, love and assistance. They are our unseen friends and protectors – you can see them as our guardian angels.

Another important aspect of being connected with other realms is that we get the comfort of knowing that the physical world is not all there is. That opens up the possibility for us to be more than we might have thought we are. In order to connect with our Guides, we need to broaden our perspective of reality and existence. Understanding that we are connected to a spiritual world supports our greatest and fullest expression.

Our Spirit Guides will show us our innermost preferences, i.e. in which areas we will be the most truthful to ourselves. An example is that if, when we were children, we found deep joy in nature, the likelihood that we will have spirit allies such as trees, the elements, mountains or animals is pretty high. Or if we found inspiration in the stars, we could very well be connected to Spirit Guides who are from the celestial realms.

Excitement, joy and inspiration come from the same source: our soul, our heart. Start paying attention to what sets off sparks in your being, because you'll know that your heart is clearly guiding you through these feelings. And emotions and sensations are the language used by our Spirit Guides. They are not literal. (Well, sometimes when we are really not listening, they can be!)

Simply put, it is in your greatest interest to look into your unseen alliances, so that you can feel more whole, joyful, peaceful, inspired and fulfilled.

How do I Learn Spirit 'Speak'?

In all great storytelling, there is myth. Myth uses extraordinary stories to help us see ourselves through the characters depicted, and to allow us to understand ourselves better. Stories are very potent; they are roadmaps. And a roadmap is exactly what our Spirit Guides offer us when we embark on a journey with them. When you start working with your allies in spirit and they start communicating with you, clues about their presence and their messages start to become obvious as you begin to notice signs popping up around you. These repeating clues or signs, or synchronicities, show that you are on the right path.

When you are on the right path, you may witness synchronicity after synchronicity. You will meet the right people at the right time; you will get offers that are supportive of your path and purpose; you will feel a lightness and a flow that will indicate you are on the right track. For instance, the flat that you wanted to live in has an opening just as your lease runs out; the person you are into is moving back to the city you live in after years abroad; a headhunter calls you for a job you wanted although you weren't sure about your qualifications for it. These are clear daily signs that you are on track.

This can be supported by other indicators that you are moving in the right direction. You might start to spot a familiar form – such as an animal or plant – that feels significant to you appearing on cards, T-shirts, in nature, or on a website. This is your Spirit Guide's way of showing you that it is supporting you. An ancestor might show their presence through old photographs popping up or if you are called to go to the region where they lived for personal or work matters.

The flow of your life as illustrated by the synchronicities in your experiences is a potent sign that you are connected to your Spirit Guides and, overall, your life purpose. There will be an ease, joy and excitement that will be your compass; when you experience those feelings, know that you are on the right path.

You will know if you are on the wrong path because everything becomes difficult. Nothing works out or, if it does, it is not straightforward and there will be complications, misunderstandings, setbacks. When that happens in your life, it is time to take a moment and pause. This is a very good opportunity to invite your Spirit Guides in and ask them to show you what is in the way and why.

How to Find Your Guides

The Universe has your back. You just need to learn how to read the signs.

I'm sure you have already said a few times to yourself, 'I must have a guardian angel looking out for me', when you've made a difficult decision that later proved to be the right choice. I call these close calls divine intervention, and this can apply to difficult relationships too; for instance, finding the strength to break up with someone who is not right for you. Sometimes we just need divine intervention and that's cool; it teaches us to trust in the Universe!

We can have more than one Guide and these can also evolve over time; some will stay alongside you for a lifetime and some will go; some will show up regularly and some every ten years. There are no rules. The way I look at it is that we are connected to these Guides in accordance with our frequency and vibration, which translates into where we are in life, the lessons we face, the intentions we set and the decisions we make.

My first guide was an ancestor, my paternal grandfather whom I had never met before he passed. He made himself known to me in 2000, at the very beginning of my spiritual journey – I didn't even know I was on it yet! He was a massive gatekeeper: he opened the door to the spiritual world for me but I have rarely connected with him since. In 2014, I went through one of the most transformative phases of my life and I still regularly connect with the animal spirits that presented themselves to me then: a Bat and an Owl. From my time spent apprenticing with Incan wisdom keepers in Peru, known as Paqos, I learned to see these animals as symbols – the Bat signifying death and rebirth and the Owl signifying seeing beyond what is shown and seeing beyond deception.

One of things you learn to do, which takes time, is seeing patterns, which will be key in your work with Spirit Guides. You will learn through observation that there will be obvious red threads. When I hear an owl hooting and I see a bat, I know a big life lesson is on the horizon, and that is OK because I know this lesson and change is for my highest good and the highest good of all. This is why I strongly encourage you to keep notes of your experiences in a journal as they will be very useful in helping you to spot patterns (see the section on journaling on page 56).

Can I have more than one Spirit Guide?

The circumstances we need support with, and the type of learning we may require, will inform which Spirit Guide will work with us. So, let's say that your current life lesson is about trusting your intuition and letting go of control. In my experience, I would be drawn towards a Guide who embodies a deeply feminine energy that holds intuition, receptivity, creativity and deep knowing, and who will show me how to integrate these attributes. So, the likelihood is that this kind of energy will present itself, perhaps through a friend mentioning a book she read, a song that comes on the radio, an animal visiting me in the garden – perhaps even a female deity's name finding its way into my daily life.

The more connected you are to the spirit world, the more your Guides will show themselves to you with ease, so meditation practice, developing your intuition by listening more to your heart (and less to your head), and activating your curiosity through reading about various spiritual traditions, or learning about your family tree and origins will lead you naturally towards the answers you are looking for.

As with the people around you, who come in and out of your life for a reason and/or a season, we are all here to learn from each other and with each other; and this is the same with Spirit Guides. They will mix and match with your life lessons.

Connecting with Your Spirit Guides

In the next section, I will give you a road map to connecting with your Spirit Guides and establishing a code or language that you can use when building your relationship with them. As with all other relationships, it takes time to figure each other out and to understand each other's 'spirit speak'.

In order to connect with spirit, there are methodologies or practices that we can use, but, first and foremost, for these encounters to happen through all or any of these workings, there must be the belief or faith in the existence of another realm.

It is good to let go of any preconceived ideas you might have when it comes to spirit, as it is an experiential journey – it is your own experience that will create belief. As I said earlier, we need to have faith in something that we cannot touch and 'prove', much as we do in music or Wi-Fi. With faith comes patience.

How can You Recognise when Your Spirit Guide is Reaching Out?

In my experience, there are two contact levels or entry points with our Guides. They can make their presence known if we need direction, especially if we are not listening, or we can reach out to them for guidance. Either way, they will show themselves to you when they have something to say.

HOW SPIRIT GUIDES COMMUNICATE WITH YOU

Your Guides will give you clear physical signs or nudges to make their presence known; especially in the beginning so that you can relate to them in your own reality. A physical sensation will help you believe and trust in their existence and it can manifest in many forms:

· some will give you a physical sensation, e.g. a shiver, a gentle brush on your face, a twitch in your shoulder;
· some will tickle your nostrils with a scent, e.g. smelling roses or cake when there is not a rose or a lemon drizzle in sight;
· some will come across as a sound or frequency, e.g. buzzing in the ear(s), a certain music or song playing;
· some will manifest as a symbol, e.g. a triangle, a circle, the infinity symbol;

- some will appear in a physical form, e.g. a feather, a rainbow, or any other form you want to ask your Spirit Guides to take to show you their presence.

We often notice their presence through synchronicity. When we need guidance and they know that our need is getting 'serious', they will start popping the props! For example, signs on the road pointing you in a very clear direction or a big fat STOP sign; songs playing on the radio with lyrics that couldn't be more obvious – or perhaps your grandmother's necklace falls out of a bag you haven't used in five years, etc. Spirit Guides mostly do not initiate contact unless it is time for you to make a move, but when we do not listen to the signs, they get bigger and bigger.

Remember, it is always for your highest good! The Universe has your back. You just need to learn how to read the signs and synchronicities, and you will gain a world of support and wisdom, additional to the one you already have in the physical realm.

If your Spirit Guides need to communicate with you urgently, they will find a way and the signs will be undeniable. It is for us to listen and not to dismiss them because they feel inconvenient or unwanted – remember that the highest good always comes first. If you keep on seeing stop signs on the road, on pictures or on T-shirts and you have just asked, 'Shall I go ahead with x, y or z?' – the message is pretty clear. Spirit will warn you when you are not heading in the right direction.

SPEAKING THROUGH OTHERS

In a programme I am working with, it is said that 'God speaks through others in the rooms'. You might be familiar with this quote, which I believe to be so true. Whatever your spiritual or religious beliefs, wisdom is everywhere, all the time.

Has this ever happened to you? You, by chance, sit next to someone who is having a conversation on the phone or with someone else, and it is as if they are speaking directly to you. Well, that is not a coincidence. (I do not believe in coincidences anyway; I believe everything happens for a reason.) Sometimes you will be delivered a very clear piece of advice through a seemingly random person. Or you might be that person for someone else, and you will never know. We are all messengers for each other and much more interconnected than we think.

Spirit Guides are here to help us succeed in life.

How to Call
on Them

When you follow the signs and listen to your heart, you can't go wrong.

The best way to recognise whether your Spirit Guides are around is to start feeling into what your preferred method of communication with them is. We have various channels of connection:

- clairvoyance (inner vision; think visualisation/imagination),
- clairaudience (inner voice; think hearing voices and recognising which ones are your actual Guides),
- clairsentience (inner feeling),
- claircognisance (inner knowing).

As you practise finding where your direct line to spirit resides, you will also be happy to know that your Guides can connect with you via other channels too.

Once we are willing and open, in order to connect, we need to invite our Spirit Guides in. Start by being aware of your general state. If you notice that you are tense, deepen your breathing and soften your jaw, shoulders and forehead. Check your overall energy and aim for deeper, calmer exhales to soothe the nervous system.

Find stillness for a minute (sit and breathe) and start preparing yourself for your dialogue with spirit. Make sure you will not be interrupted, e.g. turn your phone off and tell the people around you that you will need quiet.

Now to call in your Spirit Guide ...

Clear Your Own Energies

You should be aware of the fact that you need to be mindful when you collaborate with spirit. Spirits, like people, are not all benevolent, and if you are not mindful of the space you hold physically, emotionally and psychically, you might end up with some unhelpful guests.

Emotionally, when we are distressed, our energy field (aka our aura) can be a bit battered and bruised, so we need to be mindful of whether this is really the best time to call in spirit. A few things can be going on. If we are in a heightened state of anger, we might not necessarily have the best intentions at heart and can attract energies that are in the same vibration.

I always suggest going for a walk, or having a dance, shout or shake to let that energy out and call in your Guides from a more grounded and centred place.

Create the Space for Spirit Guides to Appear

Physically, this means that we need to have a clear place to work in. Environments hold lingering energy and it is important to cleanse it, so you do not bring any energies of argument, anger, fear or whatever else has been going down there, as it does in all our daily lives.

Always start by clearing the energy in the space with some cleansing incense and/or bells or clapping, or by burning some cleansing aromatic herbs, such as sage or mugwort – they all break up energy.

Burning herbs has been practised for centuries and more by herbalists and other medicine people to clear spaces. White sage has most commonly been used, but depending on the respective natural habitat, other herbs, resins, barks and woods can be used. Always research what you are thinking of burning as a few 'burnables' can be toxic.

If you are burning herbs, once they are lit, state your intention to cleanse the space of any energies that are not supportive. Start the process by moving around with the smoke and give corners a little extra oomph as these are where stuck or stagnant energies like to hang out. Be mindful of smoke alarms, so you don't end up more stressed than when you started!

If you do not want to use smoke, you can use bells. In many cultures, bells are thought to clear all forms of negative energy. You can use cymbals, bells or singing bowls or any kind of chimes. You can also clap your hands to break up the energy as well. Use the methodology that resonates the most with you.

A quick tip: when you enter a space and it feels a little dense, if you are able to, clap your hands in order to clear the room or the chair you are about to sit down on. On public transport, I always snap my fingers before I sit down – this sounds a little strange perhaps, but it works!

BUILD YOUR OWN ALTAR: A MEETING POINT WITH YOUR SPIRIT GUIDES

Your altar gives you an opportunity to explore your spirituality and creativity. Let it be your safe haven to which you can retire when you need holding, advice, connection, love, clarity and whatever you require at that given moment. It is a space of nourishment and inspiration.

Like a 'Meeting Point' in a public place (think train station or airport), an altar is also your rally point with your Spirit Guides. Its purpose is to create a space akin to an energy vortex where you and your Guides can set up shop for a deep conversation.

Physically, an altar is a space in a room dedicated to a sacred practice, a space of honouring the communion between worlds and beings.

First, pick a place where you can set up your altar. It doesn't need to take up much room, but it needs to be undisturbed – ideally not your dining table, for example. On your altar, you can have as much or as little as you want. It can be limited to a candle (do not underestimate the power of simplicity) or a more substantial display, including pictures of people (your ancestors or spiritual inspirations), deities, a token from the animal kingdom (e.g. a feather) or the plant kingdom (such as a branch, an acorn or flowers), a crystal or stone, or an image of a sacred place or somewhere dear to you. It is basically a space that will help you connect with whatever spirit is prompting you as you look at it and feel into it.

On my altar, to give you an example, I have a candle (symbolising light and fire), water from Glastonbury's Chalice Well, some sacred stones that were given to me by medicine people in the Peruvian Andes, swan feathers I found on a beach in my native Finland (swans hold the medicine of grace, beauty and prophecy and the ability to navigate between the worlds), various crystals, a statue of the Black Madonna that I got in Chartres Cathedral in France and a crystal grid (crystals that I have set up in certain formation) as well as a birch staff.

Ceremony and Offering

Ceremony is my favourite part of my encounters with spirit because I can get very creative in the process. I relate to ceremony as being about recognising and honouring the sacred and our relationship with it, however big or small the ceremony is – from a full-on fire ceremony with rattles to saying a quiet prayer. Any connection with spirit is actually a small ceremony.

As we give form to our interaction with spirit and build a sacred space to contain it, we officialise and concretise the meeting. Ceremonies are pretty straightforward when you combine common sense with creativity. Trust yourself – you will know. One element that is required is an intention (see pages 46–7), which will set the focus for the ceremony.

First, make sure you will not be disturbed; this is not a good time to get into a conversation with anyone but your Spirit Guides. Have some water handy, wear comfortable clothing and avoid stimulants as they will unground you (i.e. give you the jitters). You want to be present and centred to receive effortlessly.

As you enter a space of quiet, sit in a comfortable position and translate your reverence and connection to your Spirit Guides by adopting a position that shows your respect and participation. This could be bringing your hands together in front of your heart or bowing to your altar as you say your opening words or prayer (more on page 46). Any position that feels right to you will be the right expression, these are merely examples.

I personally hold my hands in front of my heart or sit cross-legged with my hands resting in my lap. A straight spine helps with the connection as it aligns the top of your head and the base of your spine, connecting above and the ground below or the human and spirit. Your heart is where the two worlds meet.

When you open the ceremony, respect the main guidelines by setting an intention (see pages 46–7), but feel free to make your own version of this. Here are a few elements to always offer your Spirit Guides:

· Give them your gratitude and appreciation.
· Show them respect.
· Pose them a question or ask for clarity (concerning your intention).

Keep the wording positive and in line with what you want to create with this encounter, so do not focus on what is 'wrong', but rather on what positives you seek. Your focus and words are powerful. And always be aware of your intention. You are weaving a prayer into being, that is how powerful you are!

MAKING AN OFFERING

You can support this with an offering which is your own creation and infused with your intention and energy. The purpose of an offering is also to give a physical form to your relationship with your Spirit Guides and to materialise your intention, making this an exchange with them and not just about taking from them.

An offering can be food (something simple such as fruit), water, flowers, seeds, leaves, sticks, stones or crystals. Prior to a ceremony, you can go out in nature and pick up items that have naturally fallen off a bush or a tree, such as a pine cone. If you pick a flower, always ask the plant for permission and, if it is a '*yes!*', offer your heartfelt gratitude for this plant gifting its life for your ceremony. In an urban environment, you can always go to the park and forage.

Alternatively, you can also get creative with what you have in your art supplies. You can offer a drawing or painting, which will also help you anchor your intention and give it form – if you want to call in Trust, for example, you can write out the word and decorate it.

Your offering can also be a chant, song, a piece of music played on a guitar, rattle, drum or any other instrument. Spirit Guides will gladly receive it all with deep gratitude.

Always Set an Intention

Introduce yourself by stating your whole name. Notice whether your body is at ease with an open heart and breathe into any tension you might be holding.

As we call in our Spirit Guide, we need to explicitly ask for help. State your needs: for example, it could be a question about a person whom you can't see clearly, a situation playing out at work, or a place in which to live or not. Focus on the positive – what you *do* want rather than what you don't.

I was always taught that one of the most important aspects of any spirit communication is intention. What is the intention behind our outreach to a Spirit Guide? If you are not sure, always ask yourself: *Why am I doing this? Where am I coming from?* One way of keeping it 'clean' is by asking for the intention to be held for your 'own highest good' and 'the highest good of all'.

One thing that you need to remember is that you will always get what you need but maybe not always what you want. It is also important to know that when we don't get what we want or feel rejected, it is a redirection for our higher purpose. Always keep your eye on the highest potential. Remember that you are here to learn, and the Universe loves you unconditionally. We just don't know it because we can't see past what is currently unfolding.

BE MINDFUL OF WHAT YOU ASK FOR

If you start asking for things based on personal needs, desires or insecurities (not wanting your ex's new relationship to work out, for example), I encourage you to take a different route to address what may be bothering you. Working with Spirit Guides is like a boomerang: the intention you put out there will always come back to you, so my advice is to be discerning with yourself (i.e. check yourself) and your Spirit Guide will align with your intention – and so will your manifestations and answers.

Invoking Your Spirit Guides

Invocation might sound rather mystical, even a little witchy! However, speaking out and naming your Spirit Guides as you call them in will support their presence and they will hear your call. Invocations will strengthen your call for a response from them.

Be clear in your communication. Like any relationship, if you want it to be sustainable and supportive, communication is key. State your full name, who you are calling in, and what you need support and guidance with. If you are unsure which guide to call, always call in beings who are of Love and Light – and ask those who aren't to vanish. It is simple and it really works; it is like setting up a buffer or filter.

An example would be:

I call forward my Spirit Guides who are here to support and guide me through life on the Earth plane. I call forward those who love me unconditionally and are of the Light in my ancestry, in the animal and plant kingdoms, gods and goddesses, nature and star allies.

Or:

I call forward all ancestors of Love and Light [always specify this, so you don't call in just any old ancestors], bloodline related and beyond, to support me with guidance relevant to [insert your need/question]. As I am held by the realms of the Earth, and all my allies on this plane – the elements, the plant and animal kingdoms, I anchor the wisdom shared and gained in my daily life for my highest good and the highest good of all.

Offering you deep gratitude for your guidance, beloved ancestors.

To invoke the Divine Feminine, you might use the following invocation or one like it:

I call upon the Great Mother in all her forms: Mother Earth, Gaia; the Cosmic Mother, Creator energy; goddesses and saints of all traditions; the elements of Water and Earth; all the women of my blood lineages and beyond who exist in Love and Integrity. Please help me remember the ancient feminine ways, so that they can guide me to reclaim my intuition, the ways of unconditional love, my creativity, sensuality and sexuality. Thank you, Great Mother, for helping me remember.

A CODE OF CONDUCT FOR YOU AND YOUR SPIRIT GUIDES

It is good to have an established code of conduct with spirit so that you can honour each other's space. The thing about relations with the spirit world is that it is a bit like the human realm – you will need strong boundaries and to be able to tell your Spirit Guide when it is time for you to connect and have a conversation and when it isn't.

By addressing this clearly, as you open your psychic space, you will filter successfully who you're welcoming in. You can say something along the lines of:

I now open this space for my Spirit Guides who support me in Love and Light, and I banish any entities that are not here for my highest good and the highest good of all.

Meditating or Creating Space in Your Head

Meditation teaches us how to still the mind, which allows for clearer communication channels to open between the worlds of body and spirit. It is one of the main gateways for connecting with our Spirit Guides. Through the space created by meditation, your Spirit Guides can reach you more easily. They can pop into your mind with a thought, a vision, a message or a feeling.

You will know that your Guides are communicating with you when a relevant piece of information – an answer – hits you. It often feels like getting a response out of the blue. It might appear as an answer offered after a time lag. Spirit Guides are concise and clear; they don't go into too much detail.

This is also why so many spiritual traditions put such great emphasis on meditating. They know that meditation is a portal for communicating with other realms, whereby we can gain a deeper understanding of who we are and what we have come here to be. Stillness, for that, is key.

We all have the capacity to meditate. You just need to find the way that works for you, which can evolve over time. First of all, you will need to find a type of meditation that you enjoy engaging with. It can be silent, sitting, lying down, listening to a guided meditation or soothing music, gazing at a candle, walking or looking out into the ocean.

In many nature connection practices I've had the honour of experiencing, i.e. connecting with the unseen through nature, you choose what is called a 'sit spot' which you return to over and over again so that you grow acquainted with the energies that reside there. And you just sit. This will help you to connect with a tree, birds, ancestors and a whole plethora of other beings. There is no shortage of choice! The most important thing is to practice stillness of your mind and connection with your body. If we are too agitated, we are not receptive or clear, and we will not hear our Spirit Guides.

During meditation, your mental activity slows down, and you become more receptive to information that you simply cannot hear, feel or see when you are in a normal state, stressed, confused or just getting on with things.

SITTING AND LISTENING TO THE BODY

Our bodies hold an often disregarded wisdom. After all, this is where our gut feeling lives. A good practice is to sit still and let your Spirit Guide make itself known through bodily sensations. For instance, one way I feel their presence is when I sense I am being stroked with a feather across my face, because that is what we agreed would be our secret handshake to acknowledge our connection – something that, with time and practice, you can agree with your Guide too.

We can also feel Spirit Guides through body temperature fluctuations; we can either get very cold or very hot. That is pretty individual. Feeling pins and needles is quite usual too.

SILENCE

Silence is vital when we want to start listening deeply. Music, even ambient music, can be a distraction and affect or influence the messages that we receive based on the nature of the music we are listening to. Silence helps to make your receptors more neutral and it makes space for messages to arrive in the same way that sitting still does.

MOVEMENT (WALKING, DANCING, DRUMMING)

There are many types of movement, from very gentle to full-on cathartic. Walking meditations help us to cultivate mindfulness, calming our minds to clear our heads from constant rumination and mental chatter. You can start a walking meditation by setting an intention relating to what you need clarity on. Once that it is set, you can let it go as you embark on your walk. Notice every single step you take and when you start getting distracted, bring your mind back to your steps. Literally feel your heel connecting with the ground, moving towards the ball of your foot, your toes and then taking off.

Staying connected with your body as you walk will help you slow down those workings of your mind that make your connection with spirit murkier. As you walk and as you let go, you will start getting answers that just pop into your awareness. You'll know it is spirit guidance when it is clear and flows.

Dancing, singing and drumming are well-known ways to get out of our heads and thinking mind and into our body, which knows and remembers everything. As we start dancing, our Spirit Guides can join in – especially when a drum is beating. The beat of the drum in connected to the rhythm of Mother Earth and the Universe. It is a good way of connecting with ancestors, animal and elemental spirits. The best thing to do is to start working on an inspiring playlist that will support your encounter and communication.

SPEAKING THROUGH ART – PAINTING, SCULPTING, DANCING, SINGING, MUSIC, POETRY

Writing is a very powerful way of letting your Spirit Guides communicate through you. Automatic writing is a particularly efficient way of giving a voice to your Spirit Guides. First, call them in and set an intention or ask a question. Take some time to find stillness and then start writing on a piece of paper or in your journal. Write whatever comes; let it flow until you're 'dry'. If you want to amp it up, you can switch the pen to your non-dominant hand, which will move the writing process away from your left-brain filter (the logical, structured, controlling side of the brain). Your page might look like it's been drafted by a five-year-old but the information will be very pure.

Painting and drawing can also be very good means to bring forth your Spirit Guides. I have always loved painting but had a long break from it for most of my adult life. When I picked it up again in early 2019, I painted something that I thought looked pretty cool – it was abstract with loads of colours. When I looked at it a day later, I could see a clear face in it! I sat with the painting and looked at the being that came through; I now know this to be one of my Guides – a cosmic being who looks after me.

You can do this yourself when painting, drawing or sculpting. Start by setting an intention of wanting to connect with a Guide so that it can show itself to you; or connect with a Guide using meditation or one of the other practices described in this book, and ask for the answer to be expressed through your art. Be sure to make your creative space sacred before you start to invite spirit in (see pages 40–2).

Singing can also help us remember that sound can link us to the spirits that reside in various realms, from deeply earthly songs to ethereal sounds connecting with the cosmic realms. One form of singing called 'Light Language' allows you to sing whatever sounds come through you; even though the words might not make rational sense, the sound does. A great example would be Lisa Gerrard and the Dead Can Dance's song 'The Host of the Seraphim', which illustrates really well what I am describing.

Journaling

It is really helpful to log dreams, insights, visions and messages. You can write or draw them and they will help you confirm which insights and messages you have received. In my experience, there can sometimes be years between noting a vision and understanding its meaning and/or receiving confirmation. As you might remember, I mentioned earlier that this is how the world of spirit operates: you take the leap and then you get the confirmation. Your journal is a great record keeper.

You might also feel an urge to write – that is usually when messages from your Spirit Guides are close, so pay attention to that urge and grab your pen. You won't just remember the messages; trust me, I've tried that and every time, without fail, I have been really annoyed that I didn't log what came in.

Journaling can help you to process emotions and make links between insights, occurrences, messages and meetings. It also helps you gain clarity.

To Close Your Ceremony and Connection

Gratitude is paramount: thank your Guides for their assistance in this process and offer gratitude for their support and guidance.

Then release your Guides by asking them to return to their world. Take a few deep breaths, connect with your body and the ground beneath you. Feel your heart beating in your chest, notice the air flowing in and out of your nostrils, move your fingers and toes and, if necessary, open your eyes when you feel ready. Move slowly and mindfully, stretch a little.

When you feel that you are back in your body and that you have completed your ceremony, get up, blow out any candles, and state that the ceremony is now closed.

Then take some time to be in silence or quiet. Go back out into the world and be aware that your energy field might be a little delicate, so take a walk in the park, have a bath, sit and journal some more with some soothing music, or have a cup of tea – whatever feels nourishing to your body and soul.

Our Spirit Guides will show us our authentic selves.

Getting Closer

The 'mission' of your Spirit Guides is to remind you of your greatness.

This is where I would like to take the opportunity to introduce a key concept. Your name holds a lot of information about you and for you on many different levels – both in daily life and esoterically. It can also link you to your Spirit Guides.

Let's take my name as an example: Catherine means 'purity' and has connections with the word 'Cathar', a Christian dualist or Gnostic revival movement that thrived in some areas of southern Europe between the twelfth and fourteenth centuries. Björksten means 'birch stone' in Swedish. I have a great connection to mountains. (Give me a crystal and I will know exactly how 'alive' it is!) I also have a deep connection with trees and one of my quests in this lifetime is to understand better the concept of purity and how to embody it. There is also a very good reason why you were born in the land you call your country of birth. Look into it: you will find clues, as you will when you look into your family tree and your ancestors.

The clues you will find in your name and origins are phenomenal. You can also find great insights into who your Spirit Guides are. These are key entrance points into deeper aspects of you.

Through Your Dreams

One way of connecting with your Guides is through dreamtime. As you go to sleep, ask a question to which you would like an answer and let it work its magic. Some people recommend setting an alarm for around 3am, which is when the veil between the worlds is thinnest, so a great time to connect with Spirit Guides and to take note of what you remember as you awaken from your slumber. It can be a little hard-core if you like your sleep, but I have found it to be a very efficient method.

The dreamscape has been explored under so many lenses. What happens when we dream? Why do we dream? Where do we 'go' when we dream? Dream interpretation has been practised since time immemorial. While our psyche is having a field trip, we can gain great insights into what is hidden in our subconscious and also communicate with other realms. Spirit Guides can show up in their various forms as animals, archetypes or ancestors, for instance. It is always a helpful practice to keep a dream journal next to your bed to record your dreams, because they usually fade very fast.

Offerings for Your Spirit Guides

In all traditions, there is a concept of reciprocity that needs to be established when we work with spirit. When we work with another human, the common currency for an exchange of service would be money or some form of barter. When we work with the Spirit Guides, we need to keep the energy of reciprocity going as well in order for us to keep a balance through a harmonious energy exchange.

If your Spirit Guides are coming to assist you, whether during a ceremony or on another occasion, you need to reciprocate with an offering. It does not need to be complicated – you can offer thanks first and foremost (as mentioned, always express gratitude), incense, food or a symbolic offering for whatever you hope to receive in exchange.

Sacred Sites

Sacred sites are geographical locations that are known for their holiness and mystical connection. You might feel a very strong draw to certain places, whether familiar to you and nearby or situated further afield. It is important to listen to that call because there is something for you there. When I felt called to Peru, I listened and after a few years of nagging I went. When I landed in the former Incan capital, Cuzco, I felt like I had arrived home, although I had never been there before; well, not in this lifetime. And what a journey I embarked on when I answered that invitation!

PERSONAL SACRED SITES

A personal sacred site could be a family home – a place where you can enter into deep communication with your ancestors. This can reveal a lot about your family dynamics and history, even long withheld secrets, which will give you much more insight into who you are and what influences you on a daily basis. It can also inform you about your talents and skills. Sitting in a living or dining room where your family or ancestors gathered could be a good place to connect with them. Get curious and see what happens.

When my maternal grandmother passed away (we were very close), I slept in her bedroom the night after her funeral. That night, she hovered above me the whole time as I tried to sleep ('tried' being the operative word because the energetic activity in that room was ridiculous!). I felt her so strongly and knew she would accompany me for the rest of my life – she is still very much with me. Momi, as I called her, is one of my solid Spirit Guides.

EARTH OR MOTHER NATURE

Nature has uncountable sacred sites; I would even extend that statement to say that Mother Nature is a sacred site in and of herself. All she displays and offers is holy, so pay attention to whichever environment and kingdom calls you the most; it can be quite informative as to what your soul needs. Do you need to experience water bodies relating to cleansing and depth as you dive into your emotions; hills or peaks, or even mountains, to connect with the celestial realms and/or get a bird's eye view on something or someone; forests and jungles to help you to learn about lushness, abundance and connecting with the grounding force of the trees; or perhaps you need the quiet and simplicity of the desert? As I said, Nature speaks.

MAN-MADE SITES

Places of worship, shrines and pyramids can also draw us to them even if we are not religiously inclined, but especially if we are. These places of worship have an aura to them. They have been built with the purpose of connecting with The Source in deep reverence; and their geographical location and the land they've been built upon can provide you with information, as well as connect you with the spirits who dwell in these places.

What if My Connection Doesn't Work?

If you wish to establish a solid relationship with your Spirit Guides, you will need to invest some time and commitment. Like any relationship, you have to participate in it and maintain it. You want to have a strong and healthy body? You know that going to the gym once or twice is not going to cut it. It's the same with your spiritual practice – think of it as strengthening your spiritual muscle.

But by consistency I don't mean that you need to connect with spirit for hours on end – it is actually much better to do ten minutes a day every day than one hour every week. Also, make it enjoyable and find ways to make it playful and inspiring, or you won't do it. Forcing things never works.

CREATE THE RIGHT ENVIRONMENT

Certain environments are better conduits for Spirit Guide connections than others and nature is the best above all else. Nature has the cleanest energy you can engage with and is also the most supportive environment in which to get spirit to communicate with you through animals, plants, trees, earth, water or mountains.

A clear home space works as well. Make sure there is no clutter where you intend to connect – clutter stores old energy and we do not want that.

Avoid opening any communication in a space where you do not feel comfortable at all costs. There is a reason why you do not feel comfortable there – your body is picking up on something that is not supportive of you.

ENERGY VAMPIRES, DISRUPTORS OR UNINVITED GUESTS

A bit like places, be mindful of the company that you keep. Choose to be around people with whom you have a clear and harmonious relationship and that you trust. This is because we can all inadvertently tap into other people's energy and start taking on their 'stuff' – and that is often not ideal, far from it.

Whenever you feel drained around someone, let that be an indicator of an energy drainage. The main sources of energy depletion are constant complaining, a fearful approach to life (i.e. everything is a disaster and dangerous), verbal diarrhoea and passive-aggressive people – you get the picture. You are going to want to stay clear of them if you want to preserve your life force and live a fulfilling life in which you thrive.

Our bodies always know – and this is very true for the spirit realm too. If you connect with a Spirit Guide that feels off, cut all cords ASAP by declaring out loud that this spirit is not admitted into your space and needs to return to its point of origin; and then visualise light. As with people, be discerning about who you let in and trust your gut instinct.

HOW DO I UNBLOCK MYSELF?

If you feel that it is difficult to connect with your Spirit Guides, there are a few things you can do.

RAISE YOUR VIBRATION

We connect to our Guides in accordance with our frequency and vibration, so if you are out of sync on a vibrational level, your communications may stall. Here are some easy fixes:

- Get a good amount of sleep as you will feel more aligned and balanced, which enhances your capacity to connect with your Guides. Your nervous system will also thank you and so will your intuition.
- Avoid stimulants as they run you down most of the time – the energy they give you is usually a fictive high that actually is draining your adrenals. When you are jittery, you are in fight-or-flight mode, which makes it really challenging to connect with anyone.
- Get out in nature: walk barefoot to connect with Mother Earth, lie down, sit at the foot of or hug trees, listen to birdsong, connect with the sun.
- Eat high vibrational food (i.e. no processed food, for example). Your body will thank you too.
- Observe your relationships: who do you feel energised by when you spend time with them and who do you feel drained by?
- Get in some movement on a daily basis. It doesn't have to be an hour at the gym, it can be a twenty-minute

walk in a park or 45-minute dance session to your favourite playlist.

GET USED TO USING YOUR INTUITION MORE

This will help you deepen your connection with your inner knowing and help you to trust yourself. Your intuition is like a muscle: the more you use it, the stronger it becomes. You can practise on mundane things such as guessing who is calling you before you answer your phone, anticipating an event and its outcome, or testing what a 'yes' and a 'no' feel like intuitively (some see or hear the actual words, some feel an energetic opening and closing in their bodies; it is for you to experience what happens and draw your own conclusions).

MEDITATE

Meditation will help you still your wild, racing mind.

TAKE THE FIRST STEP

Last but not least – and probably the most obvious fix – just start. You need to show up and be present before things can get going and start shifting. You need to invest your energy in your Spirit Guide relationship-building; but the good news is that you cannot go wrong. It is like everything else in life: it is by doing that we learn. And when we fail, we learn too! You've got this!

Spirit Guides are your allies. Always, and in all ways.

The Spirit
Guides

Our Spirit Guides take many forms and speak a language that is accessible to us all.

In this section we look at the types of Guides that might visit you. The Guides here are held sacred by many cultures and belief systems. I write about each type from my own personal experience, from my studies and time spent with wise elders.

To really understand the Guides I urge you to read widely to understand the full belief system from which they come. Consider this a primer to introduce you to the spectrum of Guides that might visit you from The Source.

It is important to keep an open mind. Some Guides that visit you might surprise you – you might feel like an Eagle and find you are visited by an Ant. But an Ant has as much wisdom to offer as the Eagle.

Ancestor Spirit Guides

My first introduction to Spirit was through an ancestor: my paternal grandfather. As I deepened my spiritual journey I started working with a great teacher at the College of Psychic Studies in London on mediumship, which put me in touch with many of my ancestors.

An ancestor is someone with whom we share a family tree. This can be someone very close to us, such as a grandparent, or someone more distant. Within families we share life lessons. The whole set-up is built in such a way that we inherit wisdom as well as, unfortunately, trauma. Through our families, we also take on belief systems based on our social and cultural background.

HOW CAN THEY HELP?

Many traditions honour their ancestors and build altars to receive guidance and give thanks to them. This practice is based on the belief that we all genuinely do our best – and so did our ancestors, so they will try to pave the way for us in the best way possible.

HOW TO CONNECT

A good way to connect with your ancestors is to get curious about the places they have lived – for example, family homes, cities and countries – and then visit them. While you are connecting with the environment, you will also make contact with their connection to that specific place.

Archetype Spirit Guides

I came across archetypes a few years into my spiritual journey after reading the works of analytical psychologist Carl Jung. Carl Jung established twelve archetypes that have become key references when it comes to archetypical work. After learning about these key references, I started seeing patterns in people and realised that most felt connection to certain traits or figures – including myself. One of the archetypes that I relate deeply to is the
Wise Woman or Healer who has extensively suffered persecution when she exercised her gift. So, the way I see it, we are here to resolve big pieces of personality with larger groups of people or collectives. There are many different interpretations of archetypes across different cultures and beliefs but, once you start looking at the familiar figures within them, you will start noticing these traits in yourself and establish which figures you are most connected to.

Archetypes are an overarching representation of a specific type of person, from the Martyr to the Hero and also the Explorer, Rebel, Lover or Creator. They represent facets of the psyche, and those aspects that we identify with on this journey through life.

HOW CAN THEY HELP?

Archetypes are templates which we can work from. You can see them as a base for a behaviour you might have adopted.

HOW TO CONNECT

Archetypes can help you to recognise those major societal blueprints that you are playing out. You can connect with these archetypes as beings and ask them for guidance on how to navigate this blueprint and then to release it or reclaim it. For example, if you fear connecting with your healing gifts, you can ask for assistance from the Wise Woman or Witch archetype. She will be able to show you where you might be blocked or bring your attention to where you've tended to self-sabotage in order to stop yourself from stepping into your Healer archetypical expression. Or, if you need more courage and to feel more empowered, you can tap into the Warrior archetype and ask it to share its energy and strategies to help you feel stronger in the face of resistance or adversity.

One way of approaching archetypes is by thinking about storytelling. If you were telling a story, which character would your archetype be?

Animal Spirit Guides

Animal Guides have always spoken to me. We humans walk with animals and their spirits as our allies, alongside the plant kingdom, nature spirits and elements.

HOW CAN THEY HELP?

Animals have been the companions of humans on this plane for as long as we've been in human form – and they preceded us on Earth. They offer us their insights and guidance, when we are listening. In many cultures, especially indigenous cultures, animals are an integral part of the human outlook on life.

During my Shamanic studies, I was fortunate to be invited by a shaman to journey (through a meditative state) to encounter my totem animal. Mine is Wolf. It came to me so clearly and has journeyed with me ever since.

HOW TO CONNECT?

Spirit animals, in general, will be quite clear and obvious in their communication. They will show themselves repeatedly. For me, this might be through means such as appearing on the side of a bus, a card or a passer-by's T-shirt. In nature, it will be in literal animal form: you might see it fly over you or hear its call. An animal that wants your attention will get it.

The best way to work with animals, is to call them into your awareness and to visualise them if this helps. When you feel them, ask them to give you their vision: imagine that you have swapped your vision or eyesight with them and can now look at the person or the situation through their lens. You will gain a different perspective. Various animal groups offer a common theme of support or medicine.

HOW CAN THEY HELP?

I now have an A(nimal) Team: Wolf (the teacher), Raven (magic), Owl (seer beyond illusion and pretence) and Bat (master in cycles of death and rebirth). Your animal Guides change depending on your experiences.

WHEN YOU ARE DEALING WITH FEAR, FEEL THREATENED AND NEED TO MUSTER COURAGE:

You can call in predators: Wolf, Snake, Jaguar and Panther, etc. Their energy can help you to feel protected and shield you. This could be helpful when tackling relationship, work or life questions.

IF YOU CANNOT SEE THE WOOD FOR THE TREES:

The bird tribe will give you an overview of a situation – literally offering you a bird's eye view. Call upon Eagle, Hawk and other birds to help you gain perspective when you feel too entrenched in a situation or entangled with a person to see what needs to be done.

WHEN YOU NEED TO SEE BEYOND ILLUSION AND DECEPTION:

Call upon Owl, Bat, Raven and Dragonfly when you feel like you are in a situation in which you need to see beyond what is being said and presented. They will help you see beyond illusion.

TO BRING IN MORE GENTLENESS TOWARDS YOURSELF AND OTHERS:

Call upon Deer and Swan, and Dolphin and Hummingbird, who will assist you with joy. They will always bring you exactly what you need at the perfect time.

FOR CLEANSING AND CLEARING:

The Frog's medicine is very similar to that of Water as it is connected to rain and it will support you when you need to cleanse yourself from a place, person or thing that is not contributing to your highest good. The Snake's medicine of transmutation is akin to shedding old skin to create a new one.

Nature Spirit Guides

Nature Spirit Guides are actually pretty straightforward –
if you think of what your needs are, these Spirit Guides will
reflect right back to you how they can support you.
Working with nature Spirit Guides is a very intuitive
process; for example:

My introduction to nature spirits really took off when
I started apprenticing with the Andean Paqos in Peru as I
was introduced to their belief that all living beings on this
earth are connected. Many Earth-based spiritual practices
engage with nature Spirit Guides and show a deep
reverence to Mother Earth. I do not know of one ancient
tradition that does not connect with the Spirits of Nature
as Guides. We are nature, we have just forgotten.

EARTH

Mother Earth is one of our greatest teachers and allies
during our time here on Earth. She exemplifies the cyclical
nature of life with her seasons, patience in transformation
and balance through order and chaos. The element of
Earth promotes peace, fertility, money, business success,
stability and growth. It is associated with the direction of
North, endings and winter, and the realm of the ancestors.

HOW CAN IT HELP?

Earth, also referred to as Mother Nature and Gaia, is often referred to as nurturing, grounding, fertile, embracing, unconditionally loving, and is associated with creativity and sexuality.

The Earth element is grounding; it takes us right back into our bodies when we feel like we are spaced out and find it difficult to be present. It is a great resource when we feel scared and unsafe. Mother Earth shows us what unconditional holding looks like.

HOW TO CONNECT

The easiest way to connect with the Earth is, to go out into nature. You can also ask for permission from Mother Nature to bring back any gifts of nature that are available, such as a fallen branch or a loose stone, but do not extract from the Earth if such a gift is not clearly available. If you take a flower, ask for permission and thank the plant for offering itself to you – because we are all one and how you treat nature is a reflection of how you treat yourself.

You could take a bit of soil home with you and put it in a box on your altar, which will help you connect with the grounding energy of Earth. You can also wear a pendant or something else that reminds you of the Earth. Anyone who is naturally hyper can really benefit from having Earth as an ally.

WATER

Water is a beautiful ally to help us transmute our pain and turn it into wisdom. Water shows us the ways of gentle strength. It can be the gentlest and most fluid element but can turn into a powerful force when unleashed. Water is associated with the direction of West, the realm of emotions, autumn and harvest.

HOW CAN IT HELP?

Water promotes love, healing, peace, compassion, reconciliation, purification, friendship, relaxation, sleep, dreams and connecting with your psychic abilities. Working with the spirit of Water is very powerful when we want to transform emotions. There is a reason why we often revere the curative waters of places, such as Lourdes in France, that are believed to offer miraculous healings.

HOW TO CONNECT

Water is, of course, very cleansing. Anyone who is energetically sensitive can benefit from using Water as an energy diffuser: do this simply through taking showers, swimming in the ocean or having healing baths (with Epsom salts for an ultra-cleanse). It will dispel any energy you have taken on from others or a place.

Water can also be used as a space holder if you are working with grief. A good way of doing this is by filling a bowl with water and writing a letter to express your unresolved sorrow. Ask Water to hold all the tears you shed while writing it. When you are done, offer the bowl and your tears to spirit with deep gratitude.

Cold water can help you express anger if you need to get this emotion out. I learned this when I went through a cleansing process before an initiation. At first, I was a bit sceptical, but when that cold river water hit my ribs and I started engaging with it by beating the water with my fists, boy, did it take off! I had no idea cold water could be such a catalyst.

FIRE

Fire supports communication, protection, physical strength, courage, willpower and purification. It is connected to the direction of South and summer. Fire is very potent. Like all other beings you interact with, treat it with great respect, and be aware that when not dealt with in integrity, Fire can burn.

HOW CAN IT HELP?

This element supports us in rekindling our fire to live a life that is both authentic and connected to our soul purpose – a life in which we feel alive. It mainly supports us in burning away whatever does not support our highest calling and self.

HOW TO CONNECT

One way to connect with Fire is by writing down what doesn't serve and honour you any more, perhaps in the form of a letter addressed to a person with whom you have unfinished business. As you put this into the flames, ask Fire to transform it – and release all parties involved.

Fire can also be an ally when it comes to manifestation and bridging the divide between our plane and the spirit world. We can write out what it is we want to call in, set an intention and ask Fire to take it to the realm of spirit, so they can assist with its manifestation. When you work with Fire, it is important to feed the flames with an offering to give thanks. Chocolate is often offered. (Yes, really!)

Fire gazing can be an interesting experience when calling in your Spirit Guides: sometimes, the flames can morph and can show you a face, an animal or any other depiction that will give form to your Spirit Guide.

AIR

This element can be represented by feathers, which is why you often see feathers connected with the spirit realms. Think of Native American headpieces, for instance. Air is connected to the direction of East, new beginnings and spring.

HOW CAN IT HELP?

Air promotes communication, travel, intellect, eloquence, divination, freedom and wisdom.

Air is also connected to the mind, our thoughts and inspiration. This element is related to the celestial and the ethereal realms, where the angels and star beings dwell. If you need assistance with being a bit lighter, gentler or more connected to the stars, Air will support you.

HOW TO CONNECT

The wind is one of the greatest manifestations of Air. If you need to clear your head and your energy field, you could go out in a good old storm to help clear the cobwebs!

Another way of connecting with Air is by using feathers and working with the wind. Observe the wind as you start working with Air: it can be a very powerful source of information when you establish a relationship with this element, and through it you will hear Air speaking to you.

Plant Kingdom Guides

The plant kingdom is a very powerful realm.

We often appreciate the plant kingdom's beauty and scents, but we sometimes underestimate how very intelligent it is. Indigenous cultures have a great appreciation for plants as healers and teachers, and are aware that they can help us to understand and cure ailments that the mind alone cannot. If we practise plant or herbal medicine, we ingest their consciousness and the plant teacher will work within us so that we can see, hear and understand matters that we are unable to comprehend with our rational mind alone.

A simple way to work with plant guidance and support can be found in the Bach flower remedies, based on Dr Edward Bach's findings in the early twentieth century. You can also explore the power of flowers with Australian bush flower essences. You will soon start to feel their energy working with you and on you.

TREES

Trees are our greatest allies when it comes to grounding. I'm sure you've heard of 'tree hugging'. Well, tree huggers are on to something. Scientists have found that hugging a tree does calm us down. The energy of trees helps regulate our nervous system and we therefore feel more relaxed.

HOW CAN THEY HELP?

Through the movement of their boughs and leaves, trees show us when the wind blows. This is a great metaphor to remember when we find ourselves getting a bit blown away by the winds of change – because trees such as the great oak stay deeply rooted and connected to Earth or, like the willow, they have the ability to bend and adapt instead of resisting the wind and consequently breaking.

HOW TO CONNECT

Feel which type of tree you are drawn to and look up its meaning. Here are a few examples of tree Spirit Guides and what they offer as medicine:

Oak: strength and endurance, helpfulness, continuity.

Holly: protection, overcoming anger, spiritual warrior.

Birch: new beginnings, cleansing of past, vision quest.

Palm: protection, peace, opportunity.

FLOWERS AND HERBS

If you've ever looked deeply into the centre of a flower, you must have seen how extremely complex they are. Flowers and herbs show us the Great Mystery, the Creator of this wonderful intricacy. I am always fascinated by the beauty of flowers.

HOW CAN THEY HELP?

Flowers and herbs have been known since time immemorial to hold properties of healing, and can be used for casting spells, inviting spirit in, manifesting visions and much more. We can often forget how powerful they are when we use them as mere decoration or cookery ingredients. I once heard that if we logged and studied every single herb, plant and flower that exists on this Earth, we would find a cure for absolutely every single ailment and illness – and I believe that to be true.

HOW TO CONNECT

The way flower and herb Spirit Guides manifest is often through their scents. You might start smelling a flower out of the blue in a context where there are no flowers around you. A particular type of flower or herb may also be offered to you repeatedly – that's a hint!

Here are a few examples of flower Guides and their medicine:

Rose: love, strength through silence, passion.

Sunflower: opportunities, self-actualisation, happiness.

Geranium: happiness, healing, renewed joy.

Iris: higher inspiration, psychic purity.

Lily: birth, godly mind, humility.

Rock Kingdom Guides

In Peru, I apprenticed with the Altomesayoqs who are highly initiated Paqos. Their domain is Mountain spirits (Apus) and the celestial realms. The reason they work with those spirits/realms essentially is because mountains are gateways to the celestial realms. I have a deep love for these majestic beings and have always felt a great connection with them. I have been blessed to experience them in dreams and as Guides for a few years now.

Mountains, crystals, rocks and stones are said to be the most ancient beings on this planet. If you think about it, they have survived ice ages, natural catastrophes and tectonic plate shifts! If you have ever visited the Grand Canyon, you will have experienced the epic might of a rock landscape. Those ancient stones have seen, heard and witnessed so much.

MOUNTAINS

Mountains have always fascinated humankind. Besides the physical challenge of climbing mountains, I believe there is something more mystical playing out. It is as if when we climb a mountain, we get closer to celestial realms, closer to The Source. Mountains are the highest points on Earth and therefore act as portals or gateways, which is why they are deeply respected and venerated in many cultures. Altitude is also reflective of the clarity of the energy that we encounter when we venture to the mountains. The crisper the energy, the thinner the veil between spirit and man.

You can start connecting with mountains and their spirits just by looking at pictures of mountains, feeling into whichever region you might feel drawn to, such as the Alps, the Andes or the Himalayas. Like connecting with birds, connecting with mountain energy will help you to get a higher perspective on an issue or a person. It can also be very grounding if you feel a bit floaty. Mountains overall (but not all) are said to hold more of a masculine energy, so be prepared to hear the truth from them. No sugar coating here. They are amazing at cutting through behaviours that we have been dabbling in for too long. Mountains want our highest good and are also very loving.

CRYSTALS

Ah, the beauty of crystals: their colours, playfulness, depth and mystery! Have you ever looked at a crystal and felt that it was calling you? Well, that is how they work: they call you. That is the best way to start working with crystals. There will be a knowing and a draw that will direct you towards those crystals that hold the properties that will work best for you and with you.

Crystals are beings in their own right and can be great Spirit Guides, holding energetic frequencies that can inform us of profound truths and healing properties. They just speak a different language, which we then have to learn to translate – as we do with all other Spirit Guides.

If you feel called to working with crystals, start with a couple that you sense are calling you. The best approach is to hold them in your palm so you can feel the crystal's vibration in your hand – it's like seeing if you are a match on a date! You will know and feel if that is the case. Another way of recognising whether a crystal will support you is if it gets hot in your hand when you hold it.

Here are some examples of crystals and their properties:

Clear quartz: this is an amplifier of intentions. It is great to use when you want to amplify a prayer, for instance, though this also means that you should be mindful of what you are putting out there and keep the amplified energy positive. Clear quartz also helps with clearing, cleansing and healing. It is a powerful stone for spiritual awareness as it opens the gateways to the spirit world. Sitting with a clear quartz in meditation can enhance the clarity of the messages you receive, as well as your intentions.

Rose quartz: this is the quintessential stone of love, gentleness, emotional healing; it helps us release stress and unite with The Source. It helps us connect with love for oneself, one's life partner, children, family, friends, community, the Earth, the Universe and The Source. It helps us heal wounds of the heart. It is a powerful stone to wear, whether as a pendant, bracelet or a stone in your pocket; to meditate with, as it will help you connect with your heart; and to sleep near or to keep in your environment. It will help you deepen your relationship with love.

Black tourmaline: this is a fantastic stone of protection and purification. It is a great crystal for diffusing negative energy and shielding you against it. When you go out and want to stay clear of negative energy in general, carry a black tourmaline with you – it's also effective if you live or work in a challenging environment. Carrying one or meditating with one can keep your energy field clear of imbalance; think of it as an etheric vacuum cleaner.

Remember to cleanse your crystals regularly as they will accumulate other energies too, especially those that have cleansing properties, such as black tourmaline or clear quartz. To clear your crystals, you can put them out in the sunshine, (but be mindful not to leave them too long as some can lose their pigmentation) cleanse them in water (although not porous crystals such as selenite because they will dissolve) or bury them in the Earth for a few hours and ask the Earth to draw out any energy that needs to be extracted from them.

Crystals, like other Spirit Guides and allies, will come and go. Sometimes you might even lose them, and they will reappear when the time is right and their energy is needed.

Ascended Masters

Some Spirit Guides who have journeyed as humans can be referred to as Ascended Masters. They are individuals who have transcended and mastered the world of the ego and material cravings, and who have become masters in their own right. They include Jesus (aka Yeshua), Buddha, and Muhammad, to name but a few.

They embody core lessons such as love, forgiveness and joy and bring great wisdom. I invite you to explore these figures; you might naturally feel drawn to whoever is appropriate for what you are dealing with.

Angels and Star People Spirit Guides

Angels and Star People are some of my favourite Guides, but they are also the ones we need to spend a bit more time to align with. They have a very high frequency as they resonate in realms of extremely refined energy. If you have always had a fascination with, and are drawn to, the stars, you will most probably have an inherent connection with Star People, also called Celestial Beings.

Angels are referred to in most world religions but who they are goes beyond the cherubim – like image we often have of them; they are celestial beings holding high levels of consciousness. They guide us from a vantage point that can be difficult for us, as humans, to access sometimes. In my experience, we need to refine our own frequency before we can connect with them on a deeper level.

Surely we can all agree that there is a pretty high probability that we on Earth are not the only ones alive in the Universe, right? Star People are often linked to a planet or constellation of origin, such as the Pleiades, Lyra, Venus, the sun, and Andromeda. If you are interested in the Celestial Beings, there are apps that can help you track planets and constellations.

I find that the best way to connect with Star People is by being out in nature on a starry night. Start to observe whether you feel drawn to a specific star – is it winking at you? Star People are very kind and compassionate and also have a very high frequency: you might feel a little wired when you start connecting with them, so make sure you ground yourself with your feet on the Earth (literally in the dirt), with some food (root vegetables are the best), through water and movement – shake, dance, whatever floats your boat to shift the energy.

They offer us a cosmic perspective on matters, so you might want to approach them with soul-related questions, but then again – who knows? – you could also get an answer to a totally mundane question from them.

As with all other types of guides, it is important to stay discerning with Star people too. Always ask for those who are of love and light and banish the rest.

Connecting with your Spirit Guides is like connecting to your heart.

Everyday
Support

Whatever life serves you, your Spirit Guides will show you the way to shine.

We have seen throughout this book how our Spirit Guides are here to help us succeed in life, and that means helping us to overcome any obstacles that may stand in our way. If you are facing challenges, here are some suggestions for ways in which to invoke the support and wisdom of your Spirit Guides.

... with Relationships

Relationships can be complicated, whether they involve family, friends, lovers or work colleagues. We can find it difficult to resolve conflicts and get our point across, or find ourselves blindsided by manipulation. Our Spirit Guides can help us see relationships more clearly and teach us how to address them for a balanced and harmonious outcome. Ultimately, they will help us relate to people with more love, appreciation and clarity.

Here are some suggestions for reaching your Spirit Guides:

· Add a pink candle to your altar, which will bring and hold the energy of love and compassion. When you light it, you will enhance your awareness of being in that state yourself, so you will attract that loving energy back.
· Take a moment to sit at your altar or in your sacred space. Now make an offering related to what you want in your relationship: loving-kindness, clearer communication, better vision or understanding of whatever is not being expressed, for instance. Write down these words on a piece of paper or get creative and find an object or image that depicts your intention – for example, a rose quartz heart, a white rose, the picture of a loved one, an image of a baby animal, or anything that will soften your heart.
· Rose holds a very high frequency energetically, similar to the frequency or vibration of Love. Having roses in your environment will help you hold that vibration and remind you to stay centred in your heart. Beyond having the actual flower around you,

you can also wear rose essential oil or rose water. This will help you connect with your heart and support you in giving and receiving deeper levels of love.

· When you need to gain clarity and to see beyond deception, call in the assistance of Owl, who has mastered navigating in the dark and seeing what others cannot see. Owl also has an astute sense of hearing that ranges beyond the norm to detect what is not being said. You can put a picture of an owl or an owl feather (if you can find one discarded) on your altar, set a picture of an owl as wallpaper on your phone or wear an owl necklace to keep the communication line going with Owl.

· When you meditate, take a moment to call in your spirit allies from the realm of Love. You can also have a picture of them on your altar to remind you of their presence and to invite their support in your quest to deepen the nature of your relationships. If you need help with clearing relationships that do not serve you anymore, see pages 117–20 on 'Finding Closure'.

· When you feel like you need some extra guidance on how to optimise your relationships, take a moment of stillness and call in an ancestor who you know modelled good and clear relationships. Ask for advice on how they did it; journaling their answer can be very insightful.

... with Your Creative Projects

When we want to create something new – be that a work project, a new relationship or a baby, a home or business – we can benefit from our Guides' supportive energy and enterprising forces, which can take the form of fertility, creativity, intuition and trust. On a practical level, you will need help with giving a physical form to your intention, so you will need creativity + fertility + grounding support from your Guides.

You can reach out to ask for help in this area in these ways:

· Prepare a special sacred space in your home that will hold your prayers and guidance to bring in the energy of the New, i.e. new life, no matter what area it is in – it could be a relationship, work or your environment. This space can be your 'gestation station'.
· Work with the element of Earth: she will hold your seed(s). You can plant actual seeds in the Earth as a symbol of your process. As you plant the seeds, say out loud what it is you want to bring into being and matter. Then water your seeds, check in on them, care for and nourish them. You can also plant these seeds in a pot that you keep on your altar.
· Ask for the assistance of Water as this is the element that sustains life. Remember where you spent the first nine months of your creation? Yes, in fluid as you grew to become the human you are now. You can put a bowl of water on your altar to hold the energy of that element. You can also pay a body of water a visit (such as a river, sea or ocean),

sit with it and ask for its assistance to infuse your project with life.

· Spring is the optimal time for planting seeds for obvious reasons, but if you are not in that season, not to worry – you can also ask for the help of the direction of East to create new life. Call in the energy of East by getting out a good old compass (most smartphones have one). Then face East and put a marker that will remind you where to turn to connect with it to ask for its life-creating support.

... with Abundance in Life

Abundance is a broad term. It does not only refer to financial abundance (which is, of course, also part of the abundance package); it is the notion that you will always have enough love, space, money and support. This translates into having quality friendships, a fulfilling job, a mutually loving and supportive life partner, a steady and satisfying income or a secure home.

In order to nurture abundance in your life, here are a few suggestions:

· On your altar, put a green candle that carries the energy of abundance and prosperity, and light it when you want to connect actively with bringing in the energy of abundance.
· Bring tulips into your environment as an ally from the plant kingdom representing abundance.
· Work with the element of Earth for grounding and bringing abundance into all areas of your life: relationships, finances and health. Sit on the Earth and ask her to support you in materialising your abundance and bringing it into your life.
· If you can, go out in nature and find yourself an oak or ash tree, as these are known to connect with prosperity. Sit at their roots and/or hug them and ask for guidance on how you can root more abundance in your life. If you are not able to get to a physical tree, focus on a picture of them or take the Bach Flower essence of these trees.

- Use the following essential oils for financial, energetic and other types of abundance. You can wear them on a daily basis or put a couple of drops in your bath. If you choose to wear them on your skin, I would suggest diluting the oil in a carrier oil (for example, almond or coconut) :
  - ginger
  - lemon
  - lime
  - orange
  - patchouli
  - pine.
- Use the following oils for luck:
  - cinnamon
  - cypress
  - lotus.

... with Finding Closure

When something in our life has run its course, we need to release it, not only physically but also energetically and emotionally. This can be following a break-up, a move or closing a business. Ending a chapter to make space for the new is very important; otherwise the old energy can dwell for a while and hijack the space needed for new opportunities to present themselves and flourish – such as a new relationship, business or home.

In order to shift the energy, you can try the following ideas:

· Take a moment to burn sage or other herbs or barks to clean up old energies – this can be the energy of a room, house, around a computer or over the image of someone you feel you need to let go. For more on this process see page 40. When we release someone, we ask for the old stuck energy to move on, and we should genuinely thank that person for the lesson(s) they taught us, as they have supported our growth. (This is always the case, although you might not realise it right now.) Something or someone who doesn't work out is a redirection towards something better, always.
· Make physical space, i.e. remove clutter – those objects and clothes that do not serve you, honour you or bring you joy. Have a little Marie Kondo (the Queen of decluttering) moment. Objects hold energy as much as thoughts do. By creating physical space, you also create energetic space to invite in the new. This process can be emotional and

if it is, good – let the tears cleanse and see them as washing away the old.

· Speaking of tears, the element of Water is very cleansing, physically, emotionally and energetically. Ask for her assistance with your clearing process – this can take the form of an Epsom salt bath or a shower or even of a swim in the wild (such as an ocean, lake or river). As you immerse yourself in the water say: 'Water, please cleanse me from what doesn't serve me or honour me any more. Thank you.'

· Ask for the assistance of Frog, whose medicine is akin to Water's energy. The Frog is connected to the rain and will support you when you need to take a break and cleanse your being (body, mind and/or spirit) from any person, place or thing that does not contribute to your highest good.

· Use images of Snake in your meditations as the Snake represents transmutation and shedding your old skin, which can represent your old belief systems, way of life, friends or environments. This is the medicine of letting go and creating a new skin.

· Call on the assistance of Bat, who supports you in the process of rebirthing. Remember that what is familiar is not always what is best for you. Letting go creates space for the new, which will remain unknown until it makes an entrance into your life. To call on Bat (or Snake or Frog); bring representations of the bat to your altar such as images or bat-shaped

trinkets (a pendant or carving, for example) and/or
visualise a bat when you call it into your meditation.
· Use sound as a means to clear energy by ringing
bells or clapping with your hands in the space
that needs release. If you move into a new room
or flat, make sure you always clear your space
and release the energy of whoever lived there
before you.
· The following herbs and resins are good for
purification:
    · cinnamon
    · sandalwood
    · myrrh
    · copal resin
    · rosemary.
· The following are powerful purification oils, which
can be worn on your skin; put in a diffuser and
evaporated in the air of the space you want to clean
up; or you can add a couple of drops in your bath:
    · lemon verbena
    · peppermint
    · cedarwood
    · eucalyptus.
Support the process by having the following flowers of
purification in your environment:
    · iris
    · lavender.
· Work with the element of Fire to burn in symbolic
form whatever doesn't serve you or honour you any
more and to return it to its source of origin. This can

range from lighting a candle and connecting with the flame to making a full-on bonfire – whatever is accessible to you and safe to work with. Always be thankful for the lessons and wisdom gained.

... with Worries and Anxious Times

When you feel stressed by overall uncertainty in your life, too much responsibility or tensions at work and/or at home, or by other sources of anxiety (which in essence is fear), your Spirit Guides can offer you a refuge. In this way, you can put down your defences for a while so that you can recalibrate and get some much-needed clarity and respite. Our fast-paced lives can put us in a state of overwhelm and that is the time you need to press pause and consult with your Guides as to what to do next.

Try these methods of connecting to your Spirit Guides:

- Light a white candle to bring in the energy of peace, purity, innocence and tranquillity, and keep this candle on your altar.
- I find that flowers and plants have a calming effect overall, so having them in your home or work environment will help diffuse anxiety and promote a sense of calm. Flowers that support peace include:
  - violet
  - magnolia.
  For peace, soothing stress and restful sleep use the following oils:
  - lavender
  - bergamot
  - rose
  - magnolia.

- Bring in the element of Air for gentleness. It has a light and soothing energy, like a summer breeze. Feathers represent Air, so include them on your altar.
- Take some time to practise mindfulness by being as present as possible in all that you do. Whatever you do, put your full attention into it: walking, when you wash the dishes or when you brush your teeth, for instance. This will train you to be in the present moment and not to allow your mind to go into freak-out mode by projecting itself into the future.
- Whenever you feel that you are getting tense, inhale for a count of four and exhale for a count of six. By taking longer exhales, you will calm your parasympathetic nervous system. When you are in a calm state, you will also connect more easily with your Guides and yourself.
- The element of Water will also support you with moving your emotions, while Earth will make you feel held, supported and grounded. A wild swim in nature will combine both elements but if you are in an urban setting, take a bath or a shower and head to the park instead.
- In your meditation, call in the animal spirit of Swan, who holds the medicine of grace, and Deer, the carrier of gentleness and kindness. They will hold you in a gentle embrace and share their soothing energy with you so you can feel it in yourself. Put an image of these animals on your altar to remind yourself of their energy and attributes when you look at them.
- Call into your meditation additional figures of gentleness and compassion such as Mother Mary.

... to Empower You

If you sense that you need a bit of support in feeling more solid and empowered before an important meeting or interaction, you need to call in the big guns. Before calling them in, you need to first be as centred and calm as possible, and be mindful of the intention behind calling forward this power.

Tapping into your power works best when you do it from a place of humility and love, as counterintuitive as that might sound. The Universe will always support us in our endeavours when these are geared towards the highest good and not only for our personal gain. When you add purpose into the mix, you will reach heights that you did not even suspect were available to you. You have come here to shine and to be successful; you just need to be aware of your intentions and decisions as to what you will be doing with that power. When we connect with our power, we are walking the line between creator and destroyer. It is a fine line where we can feel the most alive and create our greatest work.

Here are some suggestions to help you call in support:

· When it comes to feeling empowered, you will want to tap into forces that may seem intense because they hold power that is rooted in destroying everything that is not Truth or Love, which is why they are so effective. When you sit down in meditation and prepare yourself to connect, make sure that you call them in from a space of highest good – because the energy they will offer you will be rocket territory!

- I invite you to think about those people who inspire you with their courage and to connect with them though meditation. For example, I like to connect with Joan of Arc and writer extraordinaire Maya Angelou.
- For empowerment, the team you want to call in from the animal spirit realm should include a predator who is also a great protector and who channels a clear energy of instinct. These include:
    - Jaguar
    - Panther
    - Wolf
    - Lynx
    - Mountain Lion.
- Connect with the element of Fire, including lightning. You can connect with a live fire and ask it to show you where you might be dampening your power. Then ask how to step into your own fire of divine passion and creativity – the fire that lights you up and the rooms you walk into.
- Add a red candle to your altar that will bring with it the energy of strength. Every time you light that candle, connect with those feelings of empowerment you've experienced before in your life – that feeling of 'you've got this!' The sensation will become more familiar in your body and your brain will start recognising it as a default approach rather than an exception.
- Put the following herbs and resins in a little pouch to carry with you, in your pocket or around your neck for their resonance with empowerment and courage:

- frankincense
- thyme
- dragon's blood.
- Before entering a meeting in which you might need a little extra oomph or to have a difficult conversation which will require a bit more bravery, use the following oils:
  - rose geranium
  - black pepper
  - cedar
  - musk.
- And for power, use the following oils:
  - rosemary
  - vanilla.

Your Spirit Guides are your greatest cheerleaders.

Closing
Words

We have great allies in the unseen world who are a source of unconditional love and support. The main message that I would like you to take away from this introduction to Spirit Guides is that this work does not have to be complicated and you do not need to be 'gifted' to be able to access these realms and the support they offer.

It is your birthright to be guided and supported in your life – for this to happen, you simply need to reframe and recalibrate how your mind works and how you approach life. By connecting and working with your Spirit Guides, in all their forms, you will realise the interconnectedness of the web of life and that you are always supported, held, seen and loved. You hold the key to a life lived in a higher vibration, offering you clarity, life force and overall well-being and fulfilment.

Working with Spirit Guides will increase your self-belief and trust, your understanding that you are part of a great whole and that you are never alone. As you start trusting yourself more, you will start trusting life more and therefore manifest a life that supports your highest expression. The best version of you! This is what The Source – or whatever you want to label it – wants for you and it will become a virtuous circle as you move deeper and deeper into your purpose and fulfilment in life.

As a result, when you meet challenges, you also know that this is for your greatest good, for your growth, and that you will come out of them victorious as you conquer a part of yourself that was dragging you down. Faith and trust in the spirit world will bring you more joy, inspiration, ease and grace on a daily basis. Your perception of reality, your belief systems and your perception of yourself will shift on this journey to sit in greater alignment with your essence.

You will appear brighter in the world and become in turn an inspiration to others, thanks to your inner radiance. True beauty emanates from the heart. You will reclaim your wildness and your freedom. With your spiritual Awakening, you will find more conscious ways of living, truth, introspection, connection with spirit, nature, kindness, and alignment over anything else. You can reclaim your sovereignty, your power, your beauty – your birthright to be alive!

Begin to understand the power of Spirit Guides. They can come to you in life-defining moments to point you in the right direction, because that is their path and service: supporting humans on their journey on Earth.

My sincerest wish for you is to realise your fullest potential and to know deep unconditional love in your incarnation here on Earth and beyond.

Blessings

TO SUPPORT YOUR JOURNEY AND RELATIONSHIP WITH YOUR GUIDES

I ask for the blessing of your highest aspects as reflected here on Earth through your beloved Spirit Guides. May allies from all realms, in all forms, support each other in the Great Awakening of Humanity.

May you realise who you are and who you have come here to be.

May you realise the magnificence of your being and embody it on the Earth with the help of your trusted Guides.

And, so it is.

Further Reading

Crystals:
Robert Simmons & Naisha Ahsian, *The Book of Stones* (North Atlantic Books, 2015).

Nature:
Ted Andrews, *Nature-Speak* (Dragonhawk, 2004).
Danu Forest, *Nature Spirits* (Wooden Books, 2008).

Animal spirit guides:
Ted Andrews, *Animal Speak* (Llewellyn, 1994).
Ted Andrews, *The Animal-Speak Workbook* (Dragonhawk, 2003).
Steven D. Farmer, *Animal Spirit Guides* (Hay House, 2006).

Plant kingdom:
Scott Cunningham, *Cunningham's Encyclopedia of Magical Herbs* (Llewellyn, 1985).

Oracle cards:
Rebecca Campbell, *The Starseed Oracle* (Hay House, 2020).
Kim Krans, *The Wild Unknown Animal Spirit Deck & Guidebook* (HarperOne, 2018).
Jamie Sams & David Carson, *Medicine Cards* (St Martin's Press, 1999).

Incense:
Scott Cunningham, *The Complete Book of Incense, Oils & Brews* (Llewellyn, 1989).

Archetypes:
C. G. Jung, *The Archetypes and the Collective Unconscious* (Routledge, 1991).
Caroline Myss, *Archetypes* (Hay House, 2013).

Flowers:
Judy Ramsell Howard, *The Bach Flower Remedies Step by Step* (Vermilion, 2005).

Ascended masters:
Doreen Virtue, *Archangels & Ascended Masters* (Hay House, 2004).

Trusted Stockists

Supplies for herbs, incenses, altar candles:

Starchild
https://starchild.co.uk

Essential oils:
Absolute Aromas – www.absolute-aromas.com

DoTERRA – www.doterra.com/GB/en_GB

Young Living – www.youngliving.com/en_GB

Acknowledgements

I want to express my deepest gratitude to the following people and beings for helping me bring this expression of my soul through this book to life, in their own beautiful ways:

Source for my existence;

Barbara and Gunnar, my parents, who gave me life and the opportunity to exist on the Earth Plane and for all their support throughout my life;

The greatest gifts and teachers of all, my magnificent boys: Cyrus and Linus, and their father, Nael;

My dear friends who cheered me on in this great adventure – you know who you are!

My mentor, guide, friend, soul family and great inspiration, to whom I offer my deepest respect and love for her work and example on Earth and beyond, Beth Hin;

The golden ray of the Sunshine that lit up my heart;

My mystical wingman, Andreas John, who I can trust with my life in all the realms;

My dearest uncle, great ally and author Erik;

Gill Matini, Principal at the College of Psychic Studies, for her support with this book, her valuable insights and her dedication to being a bridge to the spiritual world.

Steve Nobel, amazing colleague and friend who saw my potential and believed in me at the start of my journey;

Avril Price, my first teacher at the College of Psychic Studies;

My Peruvian family, Dona Maria, Adolfo/Tupaq Ttito Condori, Claudio and Victor;

All the Mystics, Wayshowers, Lightworkers, Healers, Shamans, Witches, Wizards, Bringers of the New Dawn and Starseeds incarnated on Earth to upgrade human consciousness;

All who choose to stand for Truth and Integrity;

The purest beings on this plane: the Children, custodians of the codes of innocence, joy and purity;

I also want to extend my deepest gratitude to all the support I received from my Spirit allies who have taught me and shown that I am never alone and always supported.

Thank you ...

Great Mother, Mother Earth, Pachamama, Mother of Humanity for unconditionally holding me in love on my Earth Journey;

Grandfather Sun, Inti Tayta, for sharing your solar energy to help us illuminate our souls;

Bloodline and lineage ancestors for walking before me, your support and guidance;

Sacred plant teachers who showed me what is beyond the veil of the human mind;

Apus, sacred mountains of the world, holding the gateway to the celestial realms, with special appreciation for the Andes (Apu Ausangate) and the Pyrenees for their initiations;

Sacred lands that have helped me remember who I am;

To all who have made this book possible: Lana, Valeria, Muna, Sue and all involved in bringing my words and vision to life.

And to all I have not mentioned personally, who I hold in my heart with deep gratitude and appreciation for their part on my journey.

INDEX

Notes

Notes

_____
_____
_____
_____
_____
_____
_____
_____
_____
_____
_____
_____
_____
_____
_____
_____
_____
_____
_____
_____
_____
_____
_____
_____
_____

CATHERINE BJÖRKSTEN

Catherine Björksten was born in Finland and moved to Paris at the age of six months. Catherine always felt her connection to Spirit and people very deeply. That sensitivity did not blend well with her lifestyle and she suffered total burnout at the age of twenty-seven.

A reading with a medium at the College of Psychic Studies in London set her on a new path, and she enrolled to study Psychic Development. Thanks to her reconnection to the spirit world, Catherine's life changed completely. She left her career to study Spiritual Counselling at the Holistic Healing College in London. During her studies, Catherine found herself drawn to Shamanism, which led her to embark on a vision quest in the Pyrenees (a Native American rite of passage). Upon her return, she met an Incan Wisdom Keeper, known as a Paqo. She travelled to Peru and over three years apprenticed with the Paqos to learn their ways.

Catherine has her own private practice in London, where she works as a Soul Plan reader and Awakening Guide, drawing upon her shamanic studies, psychotherapy background and spiritual counselling skills to offer a practical approach to spirituality in daily life. Along with her private practice, she also hold sessions at the College of Psychic Studies, London.

You can find Catherine at akasha-awakening.com

MORE NOW AGE ESSENTIALS

BALANCE YOUR AGNI: ESSENTIAL AYURVEDA
by Claire Paphitis

BLOOM & THRIVE: ESSENTIAL HEALING HERBS & FLOWERS
by Brigit Anna McNeill

FIND YOUR FLOW: ESSENTIAL CHAKRAS
by Sushma Sagar

YOU ARE A RAINBOW: ESSENTIAL AURAS
by Emma Lucy Knowles

YOU ARE COSMIC CODE: ESSENTIAL NUMEROLOGY
by Kaitlyn Kaerhart